ARTEM KUDELIA PHD

Psychotherapy Introduction

(Short Read)

This book is not intended to substitute for professional medical or psychological advice or treatment if necessary. It is recommended that you consult the appropriate specialist if you require medical, psychological, or any other professional assistance or treatment.

If you are experiencing severe symptoms of a serious mental or physical health condition, the advice provided in this book may not be suitable or sufficient for you. If you have not already done so, it is strongly advised that you seek the guidance and collaboration of an experienced mental health professional or medical practitioner.

If your symptoms or issues worsen while reading this book, it is important to stop reading immediately and seek help from a qualified healthcare professional.

The author, publishers, and any subsequent distributors of this work are not responsible for any errors, assumptions, or interpretations made while utilizing this information. Readers have the sole responsibility of understanding and making use of this information.

First edition

This book was professionally typeset on Reedsy.
Find out more at reedsy.com

Contents

Foreword

Students often inquire about the existence of a psychotherapy guide that combines scientific rigor with an accessible presentation, a progressive orientation, and forward-looking innovation, while maintaining a respectful attitude towards the psychotherapeutic principles and achievements of the past.

In doing so, they emphasize their interest in a textbook that does not cultivate and develop only one approach (even if it is comprehensive and detailed!), built solely on the traditions of a single (albeit great!) psychotherapeutic school.

The need for a publication that encompasses a wide range of psychotherapeutic approaches and provides a clear exposition of the corresponding issues is evident.

Moreover, students express their desire to read not just an author who systematizes the achievements of others (even if it is done masterfully), but someone whose didactic, methodological, and epistolary abilities rest on a solid foundation of their own substantial psychotherapeutic experience.

The author of this book cannot be classified as an orthodox psychotherapist. On the contrary, they view psychotherapeutic problems through the prism of a "panoramic lens," weighing, comparing, exploring possibilities, and highlighting the limitations of each described psychotherapeutic approach.

As one becomes acquainted with the textbook's text, with its thorough description of approaches, techniques, and specific methods, one gradually realizes the thought: "Indeed, the author has tried all of this, received feedback, and reflected on it in their psychotherapeutic practice! Well, if not everything, then at least the majority."

The declarative statements and factual material of this book have been greatly multiplied by the value of that very "procedural experience" that can only be gained through conscientious and honest engagement in real psychotherapy.

Undoubtedly, psychotherapy is an art that is not granted to everyone and requires dedicating one's entire life to it. However, the author convincingly argues that psychotherapy is also a "science situated in the intersecting space between medicine, psychology, and philosophy." Yet, it is a distinct science. Scientific understanding of psychotherapy employs a different "language" from academic psychology discourse. Psychotherapy, as a science, operates with different "units" of analyzing the psyche and relies on its own logic of constructing psychological knowledge, distinct from academic approaches. Traditional university psychologists and psychotherapists even have different authorities. While the latter would insist on including B.F. Skinner, Jean Piaget, K. Lewin, U. Michell, L.S. Vygotsky, and others in the Top 100 Greatest Psychologists of Modern Times (see the ranking conducted by 1,750 members of the American Psychological Association in 2001), the former cannot imagine the structure of psychological science without M. Erickson, C. Rogers, R. Laing, A. Beck, I. Yalom, and others.

Working with this book, students (even if they do not plan to become psychotherapists in the future, which is the majority) will understand that every interaction between a practical psychologist and a client is unique. Not only the client but the psychologist themselves is unique. They will grasp that in studying the psyche, one can deal not only with a sample in which individual characteristics of the people included dissolve and the individuals themselves become "objects." They deal with unique personalities and individuality. Students will discover that the most significant psychological knowledge is often fundamentally unquantifiable, not expressible in numbers, but revealed through personal observations. They take on the character of that very "personal knowledge" described by M. Polanyi. Students will notice that psychological knowledge acquired through psychotherapy practice is, in most cases, unverifiable, meaning its reliability does not meet the criteria of reliability, validity, and statistical significance. The verification of this knowledge is based on the wealth of the psychotherapist's experience, their authority within the psychotherapist community, the number of cases in which real help was provided to patients, and so on. At the very least, enthusiastic students engaged in psychotherapy will learn to approach calmly the conclusion of V.M. Allakhverdov: "None of the fundamental propositions of psychoanalysis have received any convincing empirical confirmation" (2003).

By familiarizing themselves with the content of this book, students will be able to refine their image as professionals in the field they are mastering.

In the current era of blurring traditional positivist orientations in academic psychology within modern postclassical science, this image represents a psychologist who successfully combines academic scientific activity with practical psychotherapeutic work. They will fully understand the message of the renowned psychologist and psychotherapist Fedor Vasilyuk, who proclaimed that "there is nothing more theoretical than good practice" (F. V. Vasilyuk, 1996).The book holds great value for aspiring psychotherapists as it extensively covers the most important psychotherapeutic approaches of today. The book is characterized by:

- Incorporation of the latest scientific developments when describing each psychotherapeutic school.
- The accessibility of language and the use of established concepts and terms commonly employed by specialists.
- The materials in each book of the series are presented in a clear and comprehensive manner, following the structure of "methodological vector, theoretical context, most prominent representatives and their biography, facts that significantly influenced the development of the approach, most important concepts of the approach, goals of psychotherapy, and issues with proven efficacy within this approach, as well as the specificity of working with patients of various psychopathological profiles. Additionally, literature for in-depth study of the approach is provided."
- The aim is to focus the reader's attention on their own personal growth and awaken their interest in "trying out" a particular type of psychotherapy.

This publication and the continuation of books in the series make it easier to compare different psychotherapeutic approaches, assess their strengths and weaknesses, and recognize the common aspect that unites them all: the humane endeavor to relieve human suffering and enable individuals to attain happiness.

Preface

This educational publication explores the fundamental approaches in psychotherapy. The "**Psychology and Psychotherapy: Theories and Practices**" series extensively covers the history of these approaches, along with their theoretical and practical aspects. It can serve as a textbook for courses such as "Fundamentals of Psychological Counseling," or "Fundamentals of Psychotherapy." It is intended for psychologists, medical professionals, psychology students, and readers with a wide range of interests.

This initial book lays the brief foundation for the entire series.

Acknowledgments

I would like to express my gratitude to my psychology and psychotherapy teachers who have paved the way and established a solid foundation of knowledge. Furthermore, I extend my immense appreciation to patients, colleagues, friends, and all individuals who have directly or indirectly contributed to the writing of this book.

BONUS: Get Your Free Resources Now

I'm excited to share a **free eBook** and **exclusive access** to **psychological resources** with you. To get started, scan the QR code or visit psychemaster.com/psychotherapy-introduction-to-healing-vectors

What You'll Get:

- **Free eBook**: Explore advanced psychotherapeutic techniques and approaches that complement the insights.
- **Interactive Learning**: Engage with exercises and quizzes to solidify your understanding of complex theories.
- **Latest Research**: Stay updated with the most recent findings in the field of psychotherapy and integrative therapy approaches.
- **Continuous Support**: Get consistent tips, strategies, and motivation to assist you in staying focused and excelling in your studies and practice.

Maximize your understanding of psychotherapy!

Introduction

In the modern world of psycho-technologies, there are hundreds of different schools of psychotherapy that belong to the entire spectrum of existing personality theories and physiological concepts.

Often, a particular form of psychotherapy originates from a specific psychological or medical school. In some cases, psychotherapy was inseparable from medicine, while in others, it had its own specific theoretical constructs that could even contradict the existing biological model of human behavior and perception.

Psychotherapy, as a medical discipline that involves the use of words as an auxiliary or primary means of treatment, has existed since ancient times. Its roots can be traced back to the traditions of ancient shamanism in various cultures, which emerged thousands of years before the birth of Christ.

By employing various verbal and ritual-behavioral methods, shamans were sometimes able to create remarkable changes in their clients, whether it was the treatment of an illness, physical wounds, mental disorders, or the solution of social problems. It is precisely archaic shamanism that represents a certain form of proto psychotherapy, and it takes on different forms in various parts of the world in accordance with the cultural peculiarities of the contexts.

The psychosocial role of the **shaman** represented an evolutionary leap for ancient societies, distinguishing human tribes qualitatively from packs of other animals. In any animal pack, there is a hierarchy with a leader and subordinates, and there may be some degree of partial division of activities, at least based on age and gender criteria. Mutual aid and support can exist within animal packs in the event of a predator attack or encountering a difficult situation, and there may be various instinctive actions related to attempts at self-healing from certain illnesses. However, in the animal kingdom, even among higher primates and dolphins, there is no social role for a shaman as a being to whom other members of the pack turn for help with their problems.

The role of a shaman is multifaceted and archetypal, evolving over time and taking on new specific forms in various social spheres of activity and professions: healer, philosopher, chemist, musician, and blacksmith—roles that often derive from the shamanic image in the collective consciousness of the social group.

Originally, verbal healing had almost exclusively trance connotations without any rational basis. The shamans sang songs, chanted, summoned spirits, sought healing and blessings, and expelled dark forces from the patient's body. In the grand scheme of the ancient human worldview, which was constructed on a pre-rational, mythical level that did not rely on any foundation of rational thinking and the pursuit of objective truth, this was largely sufficient. The shaman was considered a conduit for spirits and Gods, and his words were not disputed by other members of society.In different social niches, the shaman possessed no less, and sometimes greater, power than the tribal chief, once again demonstrating the formation of a hierarchical structure distinct from that of animals. Carl Jung suggested that it was the shamanic image that became the primary imprint engraved in the human collective unconscious, manifesting in the form of the archetype of the sage—a collective group projection of wisdom, knowledge, spirit essence, understanding of the world, and the ability to heal.

The tribal shaman served as psychosocial support for the group members, reducing the level of anxiety and creating complexes of special meanings in life. It can be said that, at a profound level, the shaman fulfilled a projective fatherly and motherly role for the adult members of the tribe when their parents were either deceased or, for various reasons, unable to provide constructive advice related to their current life situation.

About five thousand years ago, archaic shamanism gradually began to consolidate, and the oral transmission of psychospiritual knowledge transitioned into a religious form, in which the role of the shaman underwent a number of changes and became more structured and cohesive.

Both the early shamanic role and the later role of the **priest** continued to serve the function of facilitating the connection between members of a social group and the realm of knowledge, wisdom, elevated meanings, and deceased ancestors, thus creating a behavioral metaphor for the neurophysiological connections between different regions of the human brain. If we were to draw an analogy between a social group and the human brain, we believe that shamanism would embody the process of creating numerous new connections among different brain regions with completely distinct functional characteristics.

The myths and metaphors in which shamans lived gradually found embodiment in humanity's aspiration to objectively perceive and understand the world, not only through the psycho-spiritual revelations of certain members of the social group upon whom the rest of the individuals were highly dependent but also through two other forms of knowledge: logical deduction and experimental testing. The process of shamanism transitioning into a religion reflected a crisis in finding a common denominator among the scattered beliefs existing within the social culture. This transition essentially created a second evident branch of power in the social sphere, thereby significantly distancing spiritual and religious concepts from human consciousness.

We can offer the metaphor that the crisis of transitioning from fragmented shamanism to a consolidated religious organization is akin to the process of maturing and transitioning from early childhood to adolescence, where some aspects of infantile perception of the world are still retained, but the organization of a child's behavior in society is qualitatively different.Formally, the beginning of attempts to perceive the world through objective rational thinking can be traced back to ancient Greece and the ancient Greek philosophers, who were able to construct rational conclusions, lay the foundations for the science of logic, and serve as vivid examples of independent thinking without subordination to authoritative proof. The Socratic dialectic can be considered a clear example of this, as can the philosophical activities of Socrates' contemporaries and his disciples.

The method of understanding the world through the prism of logical deduction and experimental experience was quite new for humans at that time, and it took centuries of attempts to synthesize the irrational and rational ways of understanding the world to arrive at a relatively common ground. Similar internal tensions between philosophers and scientists continued until the 19th century.

An interesting example of such transitional thinking processes were the conclusions of the medieval Christian philosopher-thinker Augustine, who, in one of his works, pointed out "three things that God cannot do." The first is to sin; the second is to create a copy of Himself; and the third is to create a triangle whose sum of angles would exceed 180 degrees. In principle, we believe that this aphorism can be interpreted as a form of irony from Augustine, who clearly hinted that faith in the psycho-spiritual context should not exceed the boundaries set by the laws that exist in the elementary rules of logic, algebra, geometry, and other sciences.

This represents another crisis of adolescence in the understanding of reality when a child gradually becomes aware that there are real rules in the adult world, and the ability to enter it directly is linked to the ability to let go of infantile attachments to old forms of belief inherent in earlier stages of human development. However, this period passes gradually. Even scientists at the end of the 19th century could still reluctantly depart from religious notions about the structure of the world and reality.

The realization of this internal conflict is perfectly demonstrated by the slowness with which Charles Darwin entered the scientific world with his theory of evolution. In an era when, despite the existing objective methods and objective philosophy of understanding reality in the scientific world, many scientists could persist in the ideology of the creation of the world in seven days, perceiving the religious position not as a metaphor but quite literally.

Rationalization in the scientific context gained more momentum in the 19th and 20th centuries, reflecting a specific stage of civilization's development and maturation. Nevertheless, even in such ultra-objective sciences as physics, there has always been room for myth, which allowed for the construction of new hypotheses, the destruction of old dogmas, and the discovery of new unsolved mysteries of nature.

Psychotherapy, as a **science**, is situated in the overlapping space between **medicine**, **psychology**, and **philosophy**. It has formed a deeper alliance with myth due to the problematic nature of obtaining truly pure objective information, as in physics or chemistry.

Almost all existing personality theories in the fields of psychotherapy and psychology are more related to philosophy than to scientifically established facts. If we were to list the various names of well-known psychoanalysts and other psychotherapists of different orientations, we would find that the majority of their theories are based on subjective experience. They constructed their methodology for working with patients based on their subjective experience of interacting with reality.

The validity of different therapeutic approaches began to be considered a fixed statistical fact years after the spread of a particular psychotherapeutic orientation to the general public. The response to the subjectivity of one psychotherapist is met with the subjectivity of another. And very often, one can observe a clear tendency to reject the philosophy of one's opponent more due to personal reasons than objective ones.

Searching solely for the problem in the patient's pure physiology did not provide the necessary answers. The actual cause of the majority of mental disorders is almost impossible to identify with typical infectious or viral diseases. Naturally, various, sometimes mutually exclusive, theories of the emergence and formation of certain disorders arose.

For example, Ken Wilber's integrative theory allows us to consider various illnesses and peculiarities of psychological processes based on a minimum of four basic sectors:

- "**I** - Individual Interior" (subjective/experiential "I" or mind)
- "**It** - Individual Exterior" (objective/material "it" or form/-body)
- "**We** - Collective Interior" (intersubjective "we" or shared values/culture)
- "**Its** - Collective Exterior" (inter-objective "its" social environment)

Ken Wilber's Matrix

	Interior	Exterior
Individual	I - Individual Interior	**It** - Individual Exterior
Collective	**We** - Collective Interior	**Its** - Collective Exterior

The "**I** - Individual Interior" sector is primarily associated with psychological processes, subjective experiences, and the world of philosophical ideas, which only partially reflect a clear objective reality. Through this sector, for example, we can examine the influence of psychological formations such as sexual complexes on the formation of behavior related to the symptomatology of various behavioral anomalies and deviations.

Discussing the internal motivation of an individual and commenting on the relationship between behavior and personality instances, such as the superego, ego, or id, without recognizing their dependence on the activity of specific brain regions, this sector creates a specific map for interpreting reality, which is more akin to religious myth, and the objectivity of experience often becomes a minor addition rather than the main pillar of the concept.

It may seem that the position of this sector is alien to modern science, but when it comes to psychology and psychotherapy, we find that this is not the case. Only a relatively small part of them is based on purely objective experience. A large amount of information is practically used without being tied to an objective criterion. And only years or decades later can precedents arise to make certain parts of the theory and practice objective.

Psychoanalysis is a vivid example of this. Its concepts of defense mechanisms have been used as ideas in practice for over 50 years without formal statistical confirmation of their validity. Most other aspects of psychoanalysis have suffered the same fate. And we are talking about a very large branch of psychotherapy that has been studied by hundreds of medical scientists for decades. The form of verbal therapy, based on the philosophical conclusions and observations of Freud and his disciples, determined the way of looking at mental disorders and interacting with them.

Debates regarding the etiology of various mental disorders continue to this day between subjectively oriented analysts and objectively oriented physiologists, whose opinions converge very slowly and gradually. For example, a psychoanalyst, in the course of several decades of practice, observes that people with schizophrenia develop specific relationships with their mothers, which may predispose them to the emergence and course of symptoms. The analyst can refine their interpretation and profiling skills to the point where they can confidently describe the peculiarities of a person's relationships with parental figures and the specifics of their development simply by observing their behavior for a few minutes. Their map constantly validates itself with new experience gained in their work.However, when we try to statistically and critically record this information, we sometimes find that what the analyst does is more of an art than a science. It is similar to teaching someone how to draw. You can teach someone to draw well, but it is extremely difficult to determine the specific criteria present in the paintings of Salvador Dali, Paul Renoir, Edgar Degas, or Vincent van Gogh in order to pass on the inherent talent of the master to someone else.

Similar problems have often arisen in psychotherapy in the field of hypnotic suggestion, where various researchers have tried to discover statistics on how many people are capable of entering a hypnotic trance and how many are not. What we know from our practice is that the quality of hypnotic suggestion is influenced by a significant number of criteria inherent in both the hypnotherapist and the patient, as well as the environment in which they are located. The method of work itself and the duration of hypnotization will significantly affect the quality of hypnotic suggestion.

If we want to obtain truly objective data in this context, we may encounter a number of difficulties. The psychopathological profile of the hypnotized individual is one of the key stumbling blocks. Since the depth of the hypnotic trance that can be induced in a person depends on their psychopathological profile, it can be a determining factor when collecting accurate statistics in this context. For example, based on our observations, individuals with a demonstrative accentuation of personality can be hypnotized in one form or another in almost 100% of cases, while individuals with paranoid accentuation are rarely hypnotizable or only enter a shallow trance. These accentuations depend on the activity of different brain regions.

If we create statistics on the percentage of hypnotizable individuals without providing data on how many people in the sample have specific accentuations, our data may formally tell us nothing. It may only provide very generalized information that is difficult to apply in practice.

We have observed that in many countries, the main concepts of recognized therapeutic approaches in the medical community may have a philosophical-practical inclination or contradict certain aspects of the basic traditional medical model of interpreting physiological processes. Humanistic, existential, transpersonal, and other psychotherapy approaches can serve as explicit examples.The effectiveness of therapy itself is often measured after a certain period of time following its implementation in clinical conditions. There are remarkable examples in the history of psychology and psychotherapy where psychologists, medical professionals, and therapists who have gained recognition in their field and whose methods have been approved for use by various medical institutions in many countries can center their perspectives not only on abstract philosophical concepts but also on elements of ancient shamanism and religious traditions. The theories of synchronicity and archetypes by Carl Jung, for instance, stand as vivid examples.

In these theories, the concept of the interconnectedness of various events unfolding in space and time, inherent in shamanistic beliefs, and the image of the primordial form through which notions of the divine are glimpsed, become central in different aspects of therapeutic practice.

Stanislav Grof, a psychiatrist with over 50 years of experience, describes in his books examples of thousands of his patients experiencing perinatal events. Neurologists in any country may argue that pre-birth experiences cannot be accurately recorded in the brain due to the lack of myelination of the axons in the cerebral cortex. And this is not to mention his descriptions of patients' experiences of past incarnations, which currently do not fit within the framework of the scientific paradigm.

This is what we are dealing with. There are numerous accounts of patients' experiences. Through analyzing this experience, we can draw conclusions and generalizations that can form a solid foundation for psychotherapeutic practice. However, as soon as a psychotherapist, similar to Jung or Grof, attempts to relate their findings to existing understandings of consciousness and the body in today's science, we find that complete integration is often unattainable, especially in key aspects of the theories. And we are talking about two medical professionals, titans of psychotherapy in the last 100 years. If we were to comment on psychologists and philosophers who have made significant contributions to the development of psychotherapy, we would often find even less inclination from them to seek a connection between the practical philosophy of psychotherapy and strict physiological criteria. This is an obvious fact that is often overlooked.

However, this indicates that their practical philosophy is directly related to the "**I** - Individual Interior" sector, as defined by Ken Wilber. What can be attributed to objective physiological, chemical, and other scientific criteria, according to Wilber, needs to be considered through the second sector of his matrix, the "**It** - Individual Exterior" sector.It is within this sector that modern medicine attempts to describe the majority of existing illnesses, attributing them to the activity of bacteria, viruses, infections, and injuries, while carefully avoiding abstract philosophical concepts of morality, defense mechanisms of the psyche, unconscious complexes, and similar aspects that belong to the "**I** - Individual Interior" sector.

The sector of the "**It** - Individual Exterior" is easier to deal with; it encompasses scientific facts from pure sciences. Most people consider the facts in this sector to be scientifically valid, accurate, and correct. It is within this sector that we can create experiments that can be reproduced by others. This sector does not accept mere personal observation of things that cannot be observed repeatedly by others.

For example, the work of a psychotherapist is mostly one-on-one, where the therapist, using elementary processes of induction and deduction, may attempt to map out the manifestation of symptoms and cognitive errors created by the individual and identify causal relationships between the present and the past in order to understand what may currently condition the symptom. For instance, psychoanalysis by S. Freud was created based on such observations, conclusions, and inferences.

If we try to examine it through the lens of the "**It** - Individual Exterior" sector, it would appear to us as practical philosophy with no connection to real scientific facts. However, as soon as we attempt to translate its key terms into the language of neurophysiology, it can reveal itself to us in a new, unexpected, and truly scientific guise. For instance, the concept of the moral super-ego can be interpreted as the left prefrontal cortex, associated with the ability to exhibit volitional qualities, maintain socially acceptable behavior, set goals, and achieve them. The concept of the "Id," interpreted in psychoanalysis as a complex of unconscious aggressive and sexual impulses, may find its neurophysiological parallel in the activity of the hypothalamus, primarily responsible for aggressive, sexual, and feeding behaviors. The concept of rapport in hypnosis can be interpreted as the manifestation of the activity of the trust neurotransmitter oxytocin. The sense of empathy will find its analog in the activity of the anterior cingulate gyrus of the brain, while depressive disorders will correspond to a decrease in the levels of dopamine and serotonin neurotransmitters. Anxiety and fear will be linked to the hyperactivity of the amygdala and adrenal glands, which synthesize adrenaline.Thus, we see that each sector is akin to a language of communication in which people belonging to various professional orientations are accustomed to conversing. However, the ability to view any personality or bodily process through the prism of different interpretive languages inherent in different sectors opens up a vast number of new possibilities and space for synthesizing the experiences of generations with diverse professional orientations. We observe that each sector merely operates as a language for interpreting reality, not reality itself. Even what we consider scientifically recognized facts are nothing more than a way to talk about a particular fragment of reality.

Gregory Bateson considered a sign of madness in a person their certainty that one interpretation of the world can be the ultimate truth, and he regarded the criterion of normality and sanity as the ability to use at least two different maps of reality in everyday life. Equating interpretation with reality is akin to equating a restaurant menu with real food. Following this principle, in our work, we will strive to examine psychotherapy through the prism of four different sectors, which formally serve as distinct maps for describing reality and between which bridges should have long been built. Unfortunately, the overwhelming majority of textbooks on psychotherapy currently view it through the lens of the first or second sector—the "**I** - Individual Interior" and the "**It** - Individual Exterior," which significantly reduces its meaningful aspects and potential. Psychotherapy is rarely considered in the context of the third and fourth sectors: the "**We** - Collective Interior," which allows for seeing the socio-cultural prerequisites for the formation of mental disorders, and the "**Its** - Collective Exterior," which reveals the influence of the political and economic system in a country on people's mental health and how changes in these spheres can condition its improvement or deterioration. The "**We** - Collective Interior" sector can provide a unique way of viewing the diversity of symptoms through the lens of cultural values. What may be a soul ailment in one nation may be deemed completely appropriate and normal behavior in another. Values and beliefs can not only differ depending on culture but can sometimes have completely opposite or reverse interpretations. Any attempt to understand the pathological nature of a person's behavior based on the values of a single culture (for example, Western or Eastern) will lead to a reduced and narrow understanding of the subject. Similar to the dimensions of the four basic sectors by Ken Wilber, within the cultural sector, one can attempt to form a meta-cultural perspective on symptoms and their treatment, not based on the ideology of a single culture but by comparing one culture to another and trying to understand which system of therapeutic beliefs may better correspond to different ethnic characteristics. Such integration into a meta-positive position is, in my opinion, a natural evolutionary step in the development of the psychotherapeutic process.

The position of theoretical synthesis will primarily aim to create a kind of Integrative Operational System within the psychotherapist's consciousness, enabling the practical integration of theoretical developments in completely different areas of activity and finding ways to shape the psychotherapeutic process at various levels: psychological, philosophical, medical, chemical, cultural, sociological, economic, and political.

The subject matter of the fourth sector—the "**Its** - Collective Exterior" for psychotherapy—is somewhat of a "dark forest," yet it is precisely the state of a large social system in a country that fractally reflects the health of smaller fractals within the system, such as the sum of cultures existing in the country, families within different cultures, and individuals within the family system. The fractal organization of this structure can provide not only a unique perspective and multidimensional perception of the problem context but also enable the transfer of practical methods from one context to another.

Let's consider a vivid example: Few people realize that the relationships between the leader of a large system and their subordinates generally reflect the psychodynamics of each family system belonging to the larger system. The attitude towards the father figure in a family extends to the male boss in a company; colleagues often project sibling transferences if the individual has any, and subordinates may reflect children's dynamics. This is a highly generalized model of representation in which there are numerous interpretative criteria, but the direction of attention alone can create an entirely new methodology for relationships. In such a methodology, a psychotherapeutic method aimed at correcting the neurotic condition of an individual can lead to constructive changes, for example, in the economic and political state of the country. This may initially sound utopian, but in our work, we will strive to conduct a detailed analysis of the possibility of drawing such parallels, which makes this work interesting not only for psychologists, psychotherapists, and medical professionals but also for a wide range of readers.

The next issue we will address in the context of this book series is the positioning of verbal psychotherapy as a distinct professional path that is only partially related to medicine, psychology, sociology, philosophy, anthropology, and cybernetics. More precisely, it has direct relevance to them but at the same time, it stands apart from them.

As we have come to realize from Ken Wilber's concept, the process of education in the psychology faculty pays much more attention to the "**I** - Individual Interior" sector, while in medical school, it focuses on the "**It** - Individual Exterior." A psychologist will have philosophical notions about symptoms, whereas a medical professional will focus on physiological aspects. An anthropologist will provide us with abundant information from the cultural context "**We** - Collective Interior," while legal experts and economists will contribute from the broader social perspective "**Its** - Collective Exterior."

In our view, it is only through the integration of multiple sectors that we can arrive at the most effective methods of work. Therefore, it is necessary to establish the profession of psychotherapist as a separate category, encompassing the best aspects related to this subject from psychology, medicine, philosophy, and other disciplines while excluding topics unrelated to psychotherapy within those disciplines. To the best of our knowledge, such separation and segregation of the psychotherapist profession are gradually being implemented in some universities in various Western countries. The pace at which this trend will reach other regions of the world is unknown, but in my opinion, at least theoretical attempts should be made to initiate movement in this direction.Another interesting piece of evidence supporting this concept is that some renowned leaders and creators of various psychotherapy methods are medical professionals, while others are psychologists. On the one hand, we can observe the tendency of medical professionals to confine psychotherapy strictly within their realm of competence. However, paradoxically, we also witness the same medical professionals applying methods and techniques developed by psychologists in clinical settings. I have witnessed numerous such situations. In this case, it is clearly necessary to abandon double standards and recognize the specificity of psychotherapeutic knowledge as interdisciplinary and integrative.

In this work, I would like to apply a slightly unconventional approach to exploring the main themes of psychotherapeutic science. Most often, textbooks on general psychotherapy simply provide a list of existing therapeutic schools: who created them, what is their history of development, and what are their basic theoretical concepts and technical arsenal? Their analytical comparison and the evident fact that different types of psychotherapy are more suitable and appropriate for treating certain disorders while less suitable for others are usually overlooked. Another problem is the criteria for selecting which directions in psychotherapy to include in the textbook, considering that as of 2000, over 700 directions in psychotherapy were registered worldwide. A textbook is not elastic, and typically, it can adequately accommodate only 10–15 of the most popular directions, with brief mentions of some others. I have chosen a slightly different style of presentation, where we examine vectors of psychotherapy within the books of the series instead of focusing on specific directions.

In my view, a vector represents a category that can include a group of therapeutic directions sharing key values and beliefs, forming the basis for the theoretical framework and technical arsenal of a particular method. Many dozens of different therapy schools can be encompassed within a single psychotherapeutic vector.

Conversely, one therapy school may utilize different vectors. A simple example would be the cognitive and behavioral vectors, which employ entirely distinct theoretical and practical foundations. However, the resulting intersection of these schools, such as cognitive-behavioral therapy, can be interpreted through the prism of both corresponding vectors.

Some integrative forms of psychotherapy, like NLP-psychotherapy, can integrate almost all known vectors, allowing for the application of multidisciplinary psychotherapeutic methodologies. On the other hand, we can observe schools that are exclusively tailored to one psychotherapeutic vector, rejecting the methodologies of others. Whether this is good or bad remains a philosophical question.However, in our work, which aims to adopt an integrative approach to the diversity of experiences, we will accept and consider all existing paradigms in psychotherapy as viable and acceptable to varying degrees. At the same time, one significant factor is the personality of the psychotherapist who applies a given method, filtering and refracting it through the lens of their own personality.

In this work, we will emphasize eleven fundamental vectors of psychotherapy, which, in my opinion, are divided into five dichotomies, reflecting the fact that the conceptual basis of some vectors has a diametrically opposite focus of attention compared to others.

Furthermore, one book of the series will be dedicated to the integrative and eclectic vector in psychotherapy, capable of uniting different theoretical and practical knowledge accumulated in various psychotherapy schools.

The first such dichotomy is the psychoanalytic and hypnotic vectors in psychotherapy.

Psychoanalytic and Hypnotic Approaches

The psychoanalytic vector in psychotherapy emphasizes mindfulness and conscious introspection of past experiences. It focuses on analyzing the dynamics of morality and instinct in consciousness and behavior, rejecting suggestion as a primary therapeutic method. On the other hand, the hypnotic vector, in its original form, prioritizes suggestion as the main catalyst for change and often overlooks psychodynamics and preceding trauma in relation to symptoms. Some practitioners attempted to merge analytical principles with hypnosis, leading to the development of methods like hypnoanalysis. However, conflicts emerged as different practitioners held opposing views and approaches.

For instance, Pierre Janet, an opponent of Freud, employed hypnoanalysis to work with a young girl experiencing painful menstrual periods. Through hypnotic regression, Janet discovered that the girl associated her first period with something bad and dirty. In an extreme attempt to relieve the pain, she immersed herself in cold water. Although her periods ceased temporarily, they returned as heavy and painful when she was 15. Janet decided to implant false memories by suggesting that she had only stood next to the barrel during that incident. Surprisingly, the pain syndrome disappeared during her next menstrual period. Janet's unconventional approach sparked controversy, with critics accusing him of practicing therapy through lies, contrasting it with Freud's emphasis on acknowledging the truth.

Non-analytically oriented hypnotherapists often construct hypnotherapy based on suggestion, guiding the patient from the problematic context to an opposite state. Hypnotherapist K. K. Platonov, for example, describes a case where he induced a severely depressed man, whose wife had left him, into a hypnotic state. Platonov then suggested that the patient should redirect his attention to the future, stop thinking about his ex-wife, seek a new partner, and find joy in life. This approach disregards psychoanalytic psychodynamics entirely. Nevertheless, practitioners like Platonov have reported successful hypnotic interventions and observed long-term positive dynamics in their patients, validating the effectiveness of their work.

The existence of contradictory beliefs and practices in different psychotherapy systems highlights the challenge of determining absolute truth. Ken Wilber, through a comparative analysis of various schools of psychology and psychotherapy, proposes an integrative model that accepts different, sometimes conflicting, beliefs as elements of a spectrum. Each therapeutic approach possesses its own validity within a specific range of meanings. Like different colors of a rainbow, various theories and practices in psychotherapy serve as maps, each representing a unique perspective. When viewed collectively, they offer different lenses through which to understand the world, contributing to a common meta-meaning.

In conclusion, the field of psychotherapy encompasses diverse approaches and perspectives, each with its own value and relevance. The integrative model encourages the utilization of various therapeutic theories and techniques, similar to different medical treatments that prove most effective when applied in appropriate contexts. Recognizing that each theory represents a piece of the broader psychotherapeutic landscape allows for a comprehensive understanding and application of different approaches.

Provocative and Humanistic Therapies

Humanistic psychotherapy, created by Carl Rogers as an alternative to authoritarian psychoanalysis and behaviorism, became part of the broader humanistic movement in America in the mid-1960s and early 1970s. This period witnessed a gradual rejection of segregation based on race and sexual orientation. It was a time of hippies, LSD-25, marijuana, and a refusal to participate in the military in favor of love and world peace. Practices such as yoga, Buddhism, and Hinduism gained popularity. Overall, it was a tangible manifestation of democracy.

Rogers changed the term "patient" to "client," metaphorically comparing psychotherapy to a dance in which the client leads. He believed that all the necessary resources for change already exist within the client, and the therapist's role is simply to provide conditions of acceptance, warm support, and tissue paper. These changes were widely accepted and became particularly popular as they embodied the spirit of humanization.

However, the limitations of humanistic methods in addressing severe neurotic and psychotic disorders were soon realized. Nonetheless, the humanistic approach was crucial at that time to counter the oppressive nature of authoritarianism in psychotherapy and introduce a new element into the spectrum of therapeutic communication. Paradoxically, this rebellion within the humanistic tradition gave rise to another rebellion, led by a figure named Frank Farrelly.

Farrelly, a psychiatrist, began experimenting with deliberately non-humanistic methods, which he later referred to as "provocative." He infused humor and irony into psychotherapy, turning therapy sessions into unique stand-up acts. He eliminated pompousness but reintroduced authority in a sarcastic manner, finding that many humanistic principles, such as empathy, acceptance, and respect, when turned inside out, could yield remarkably strong and original results. Contrary to expectations, he emphasized the contradictory and multifaceted nature of human beings.

Independently of Farrelly, the American hypnotherapist Milton Erickson also employed provocative methods, albeit in a different way. Erickson primarily used provocative situations or assignments that involved specific post-hypnotic suggestions, rather than engaging in direct provocative dialogue with his patients. While Farrelly openly challenged schizophrenics in hospitals, provoking them to realize that there are people even more insane than themselves, including their psychiatrist, Erickson would adapt to an aggressive girl in a ward, joining her in tearing apart bed sheets and ripping the heating radiator from the wall. Then, in agreement with the nurse, he would tear off the girl's gown in the corridor, provoking her to exclaim that such behavior is likely not allowed. The styles differ slightly, but the essence remains the same. It is worth noting that Erickson never referred to his method as "provocative."

Another notable dichotomy, both in terms of meaning and approach, can be observed between behavioral psychotherapy on one side and existential psychotherapy and transpersonal therapy on the other. While the latter is not a mere copy of the former, it largely embodies the same spirit of psychotherapy, exploring philosophical, abstract, spiritual, and transpersonal realms.

Behavioral and Existential, Transpersonal Therapies

Here we can gradually begin to note that the overwhelming majority of psychotherapy approaches emerged in opposition to their predecessors. Psychoanalysis emerged as a rebellion against hypnotic suggestion, behaviorism as a rebellion against psychoanalysis, humanism as a rebellion against psychoanalysis and behaviorism, and the existential and transpersonal movements as a rebellion against the excessive materialism of psychoanalysis and behaviorism. It is difficult not to recognize that opposition is the driving force behind progress. However, until it starts to seriously contradict objective reality by asserting that the methodology of one school is true and all others are harmful, it remains a valid point. It should be added that the opposition between two other approaches—cognitive and somatic—can significantly influence an individual's mental state. Cognitive therapists focus on cognitive errors made by people in the thinking process, while somatic psychotherapists become preoccupied with releasing the patient's muscular armor and assisting in the expression of various suppressed emotions that form the basis of neurotic and even psychotic processes.Behavioral therapy formally began with an experiment conducted on an 11-month-old boy named Albert. This experiment resembled a form of abuse, and it is unlikely that it could be conducted in the modern scientific world for ethical reasons. The boy was shown a white rat and then subjected to strong, fear-inducing strikes on a metal gong behind him. After a certain number of repetitions of this procedure, the boy started crying at the sight of the rat without the gong strikes. His negative reactions extended to inanimate, white, fluffy objects.

Scientists have concluded that the reverse process is possible, and they are capable of instilling positive states into previously recorded negative reactions. All of this is in line with the philosophy of radical behavioral reductionism, which denies the existence of anything in consciousness that cannot be seen, heard, or felt. Reductionist behavioral theories in psychotherapy found their place largely thanks to the ultra-objective theories of this method and the ability of these methods to bring about actual changes in the personalities of patients. However, without taking into account the multidimensionality of personality, the value-motivational apparatus, the goals of the individual, and their emotions, the behavioral method could sometimes transform from psychotherapy into a rather sophisticated form of abuse. This happened in the 1950s with aversive-reversive therapy, which was actively attempted in Europe and America for the treatment of homosexuality. At that time, individuals accused of homosexuality were given the opportunity, or rather forced, to undergo aversive-reversive therapy, in which they were induced to vomit and subjected to electric shocks while being shown images of naked people of the same sex as themselves and then forced to masturbate to images of people of the opposite sex. If we consider this method now, it is quite easy to conclude that success in some cases is possible only if the homosexual individual consciously desires to reshape their symptoms. However, this procedure, as far as we know, was often involuntary. Moreover, the coercive format not only failed to change a person's sexual orientation but could also lead to significant additional problems.

Currently, some outdated behavioral methods are still being used in certain clinics. However, more often than not, this approach is combined with other styles of psychotherapy, such as cognitive and hypnotic techniques.The existential and transpersonal dimensions of psychotherapy focus on exploring deep philosophical and psycho-spiritual meanings that exist within the patient's personality (if such meanings can be discovered). Although each dimension touches upon slightly different sectors of therapeutic work, existential therapy primarily emphasizes the attempt to create a special high-level abstract meaning of life that can organize the individual's personality and enable more effective regulation of emotional states.

The awareness of beliefs and values related to death, isolation, freedom, inner emptiness, love, and wholeness permeates the existential approach, transforming the psychotherapeutic session into a philosophical conversation—an intricate, sophisticated, and sometimes elevated discourse, which, however, often remains inaccessible to certain clients due to either their low intellectual level or underdeveloped abstract thinking, which are frequently synonymous. Human rationality is directly linked to the ability to generalize acquired information through experience or observation into abstract categories. The great meaning of life reflects these abstractions.

For some individuals, an abstract understanding of life must be reached independently through conversation and reflection. Others yearn for the sharing of abstract concepts by those around them. This should simply be accepted as an objective reality. Consequently, it is rare to find existential psychotherapy applied in clinical settings where rapid and clear procedures are necessary to accommodate the flow of patients. Moreover, it should be noted that the existential dimension is often absent from these procedures. Instead, there are specific meanings that require attention and rules of interaction with the patient to achieve the desired effect.

Some authors who pioneered existential psychotherapy gained their experience and insights under harsh circumstances. For instance, Viktor Frankl, an Austrian psychiatrist, neurologist, and psychologist, was imprisoned in three Nazi concentration camps from 1942 to 1945. During his time in the camps, he devoted almost all his efforts to assisting fellow inmates while secretly working against the Nazis. In such conditions, Frankl discovered that people are driven and maintain their will to live not only by their sexual desires or the pursuit of power but also by the search for meaning in their existence, which becomes a determining factor for survival on the brink of life and death. Frankl believed that an objective perspective on the suffering endured could help individuals survive in difficult situations. In 1945, he was liberated from the concentration camp by Allied forces, and in 1946, he became the head of the Vienna Neurological Clinic. The work he did in the camp provided him with a strong impetus for the development of his theory, which he successfully put into practice.Despite the remarkable theoretical and philosophical developments in existential therapy, in our subjective opinion, it is only applicable to a portion of patients who are willing to undergo change on a high philosophical and abstract level. At the same time, it is essential to acknowledge that the pure application of various psychotherapeutic approaches can yield similar results: good applicability to individuals possessing a particular personality profile, while showing almost complete inadaptability to representatives of other profiles.

A striking example of such a mismatch can be found in some theories of gestalt psychotherapy, where its founder, Frederick Perls, encountered patients with schizoid profiles—individuals who primarily live through cognitive processes rather than bodily sensations and emotions—and referred to them as "paper people," often refusing to work with them as a result. Sigmund Freud set very high intellectual requirements for undergoing psychoanalysis. In the realm of hypnotic suggestion, individuals suffering from paranoid disorders often do not receive the necessary help. Hypnotherapists, with great sympathy and enthusiasm, will speak more about hysteroid and demonstrative personalities than about paranoids, who, in 99% of cases, are incapable of entering a full hypnotic state.In an attempt to create a map of an integrative theoretical approach in psychotherapy, we have discovered that different approaches correspond well to different psychopathological profiles and are largely oriented towards some of them. Understanding this correlation can be a great help in forming a complex set of meta-beliefs that reveal the methodology of the correct profile-based application of therapeutic toolsets inherent in various schools of psychotherapy. In our work, we will pay much attention to this theme so that the reader can grasp key concepts about the combination of methods with different profile characteristics. However, it is worth emphasizing that it is not the vector or school of psychotherapy that engages in treatment but rather the doctor, psychologist, or philosopher who filters the method through the prism of their own personality. The personal factor in psychotherapy greatly influences the process and must be taken into account.

In the transpersonal vector, we can see attempts to integrate Western and Eastern philosophies into a unified concept that can be applied for psychotherapeutic purposes. In this vector, the attitude towards ancient forms of philosophy and religion is based on the perception of them as different forms of protopsychology and their ability to partly serve as theoretical and practical foundations for this method of psychotherapeutic practice. Due to this, the methodology of transpersonal psychotherapy may deviate from notions of rationality and scientificity. Although at times the excessive esotericism of transpersonal psychotherapy is nothing more than an alternative description of reality, it can suit individuals who share it perfectly.

The module in psychotherapy associated with the transpersonal aspect was established by Carl Gustav Jung, who started propagating his concepts about the collective unconscious and its archetypes in the early 20th century. Jung describes an interesting case from his practice when he worked at the Burghölzli Clinic. One patient suffering from schizophrenia beckoned him to the window, pointed at the sun, and began talking about seeing a solar phallus hanging from the sun and being surrounded by a solar wind.

Jung remembered his patient's strange fantasies and returned to them about five years later. Archaeologists discovered a hidden library in Egypt, and the manuscripts found there were sent to various scholars for research. Several such manuscripts ended up in the hands of Carl Jung.

In one of the manuscripts, Jung found a description of an ancient ritual performed by a priest of the Mithras cult, which was active in the East before the rise of Christianity. In this description, Jung found phrases that perfectly matched the schizophrenic patient's fantasies from Burghölzli. It depicted the sun that he was looking at, the solar phallus hanging from it, and the solar wind blowing it.For Jung, this situation was similar to the story of Isaac Newton, who had an apple fall on his head and, according to legends, "discovered" the gravitational force of the Earth. After this incident, Jung began to discover that what had previously been considered the nonsensical delusions of mentally ill individuals could be very clear material, which the patients themselves most likely couldn't have known with a high probability.

Jung observed many similar coincidences, which led him to actively study religion and alchemy in order to effectively recognize and find correspondences between the experiences of patients and the structural elements of myths and legends. Later, Jung discovered that the collective unconscious could actively manifest itself through the prism of dreams, which could be subjected to analysis.

However, Jung never referred to his work as transpersonal psychotherapy. One of the formal pioneers of both transpersonal psychology and psychotherapy can be considered Stanislav Grof, who, as a medical doctor and Freudian psychoanalyst, came to a similar understanding and representation of the intrapersonal processes of patients while working with holotropic breathwork. Observing the states described by patients after undergoing holotropic psychotherapy, he became increasingly convinced of Jung's correctness, his concepts of the collective unconscious, and the manifestation of archetypes in each individual. The key was the altered state of consciousness during mental illness, patients' dreams, or other altered states of consciousness produced by specific breathing techniques.

The anti-psychiatric vector has a strong inclination towards existential philosophy. It pays a lot of attention to the idea of illness as an alternative form of health that has not found constructive socialization.

Cognitive and Somatic Therapies

The creator of cognitive psychotherapy is Aaron Beck, who introduced the concept that patients create certain cognitive errors in their thinking process, distorting their behavior and the states they experience. Cognitive psychotherapy aims to change and transform such incorrect and illogical thoughts and beliefs in individuals, as well as various forms of stereotyping that may occur in perception. A cognitive psychotherapist can help a patient reformulate old thinking strategies or develop better ones that lead to more constructive, positive states and personal balance. Unlike psychoanalytically oriented therapists, cognitive psychotherapists pay much less attention to early childhood experiences and focus the therapy process on the present. The way you think and perceive reality at this moment is the primary focus of attention in their work. In my opinion, cognitive psychotherapy and its methods are more effective as a complement to psychoanalytic work than contradicting it. Aaron Beck's cognitive therapy is one of the most recognized in the scientific community and finds wide application in clinical practice.

Albert Ellis's Rational-Emotive Therapy, which developed separately and independently from Beck's cognitive psychotherapy, largely duplicates its key focuses of attention and principles of work. Ellis placed much more emphasis on finding cognitive process characteristics universal to all disorders, while Aaron Beck tried to differentiate different pathological conditions based on the content of cognitive processes.

An interesting psychotherapist who significantly developed and complemented the methods of cognitive therapy is Donald Meichenbaum, who, in his works, sought to draw on the ideas of L.S. Vygotsky and A.R. Luria. He created a specific method of self-instructions based on the use of inner dialogue to balance behavioral reactions. He applied this method to reshape the behavior of children with hyperactive and impulsive behaviors. In his research, he attempted to teach schizophrenic patients to engage in a "healthy conversation" by modifying their cognitive patterns. The initial stages of this process involved a symbol-digit test and the Porteus Maze Test of non-verbal intelligence. Patients gradually learned to use self-regulating statements in their everyday lives. As one set of skills was consolidated, new exercises were introduced, such as proverb tests and interviews. Meichenbaum taught his patients to first evaluate their behavior on a specific scale and then, if the assessment was unsatisfactory, instruct themselves to achieve the desired comfortable behavior.

The somatic direction in psychotherapy originated with one of Sigmund Freud's disciples, Wilhelm Reich, who initially worked using traditional Freudian concepts of the psychoanalytic process and later began developing his own theoretical and practical concepts for conducting psychotherapy.

Wilhelm Reich's theory of muscular armor has become one of the fundamental concepts in most branches of body-oriented psychotherapy. Reich viewed any neurotic process and its associated defense mechanisms, such as repression, suppression, and denial, as a complex of muscular tensions existing within the body. These tensions are caused by emotions, states, experiences, and desires that have been suppressed at various stages of the patient's life. The therapist's goal in this case was to gradually release this tension, aiming to form a balanced, or, as Reich called it, genital personality. The emphasis on genitality was largely connected to Reich's belief that sexual suppression is the key process leading to neurosis. However, Reich also considered seven zones in the human body that, to varying degrees, can block the expression of different emotions and states through their tension.

Later on, Reich began developing various new concepts, such as the theory of orgone energy existing in the human body, which, in theoretical terms, closely resembled Anton Mesmer's concept of magnetic fluid transmitted from the mesmerist to the patient for the purpose of healing.

Reich even designed specific devices intended to accumulate and transmit this energy to patients. However, such an invention was not recognized within the scientific community.

Wilhelm Reich's personality, like many of his inventions, is ambiguous. Nevertheless, it is clear that his works made a significant contribution to the development of psychotherapy in general and its body-oriented forms in particular.

Numerous direct and indirect disciples of Wilhelm Reich continued the development of his theoretical concepts and practical methods. Among the most well-known are Franz Alexander, the creator of psychosomatic psychoanalysis, as well as Alexander Lowen, the founder of bioenergetic analysis, Marion Rosen, the founder of the Rosen Method, and Ida Rolf, the creator of Rolfing.

In addition to Wilhelm Reich, an interesting method of body

physiotherapy and psychotherapy was developed by physicist and judo practitioner Moshe Feldenkrais. His method initially originated as an attempt at self-physiotherapy when, after refusing surgery on his injured knee, he began independently developing rehabilitation techniques and conscious movement. After some time, he started sharing his discoveries with colleagues and others, conducting lectures and training courses related to the topic of rehabilitation. His restorative practice allowed him to return to judo training at the Budokwai dojo in London. Over time, his method found its place both in clinical physio-rehabilitation and body-oriented psychotherapy.

The Feldenkrais Method provides a unique opportunity to work with the muscular framework of the human body in a special way. Feldenkrais discovered that by working with slow movements and minimal physical intervention on the body and its specific segments, tensions hidden within the body can be quickly and effectively released, subsequently revealing the emotions existing behind the muscular framework. Some exercises of the method can be performed as dynamic individual exercises, while others require the practitioner to work directly with the patient.

At first glance, it may seem that the method is not capable of bringing anything exceptional to the transformative dynamics of the mind and body. However, the effectiveness of the method can indeed be remarkable, and brief manipulation of the patient's body can serve as a catalyst for personality change. It is unlikely, however, that this method can fully replace the psychotherapeutic process; rather, it can serve as an excellent complement and instrumental foundation for transformative body practices.

Each body therapy method possesses its own unique qualities

and characteristics, but ultimately, they utilize similar principles that allow for the exploration of various facets of a person's mental and physical potential.

Psychodrama and Pharmaceutical, Psychedelic Therapies

The starting point for drama therapy in psychotherapy can be traced back to the beginning of the 20th century when, independent of other psychotherapeutic traditions, the psychologist, psychiatrist, and sociologist Jacob Moreno created an original method of psychotherapy based on the theatrical context. This context provides an opportunity to integrate multi-level communication into the practice of psychotherapy, implying a deeper level of self-communication, more precisely, with different parts of one's own personality. It enables the ability to establish a specific type of contact with various group participants in a form that is not accessible in ordinary social communication, allowing the expression of emotions that are usually not fully conveyed. It facilitates a dissociated, detached understanding of the current life context and enables a higher level of awareness.

Additionally, as the creator of the method, Jacob Moreno stated, "to encounter the world in both its social and cosmic meanings." Presumably, by the term "cosmic meaning," Moreno meant the attainment of changes in personality at more abstract and global levels that can transform a person's identity, rather than just a specific pattern of reaction.

Moreno named his therapy method "psychodrama," which translates literally as "the action of the soul." The key distinction between psychodrama and other methods was that it was not a typical conversational form of psychotherapy. The essential aspect of the transformative therapeutic process was the observed or performed action.The psychodramatic format of work, in many ways, became an opposition to other therapeutic methods of that time and formed a matrix of therapeutic interaction of an entirely different type. Based on this matrix, similar forms of psychotherapy were subsequently developed, relying on a dramatic mode of work. According to Moreno, the most similar types of psychotherapy to psychodrama are Virginia Satir's "family sculpture" and Bert Hellinger's "family constellations," which may significantly differ in their theoretical and practical foundations. These methods should not be classified as imitative since their literal adoption was either incomplete or absent altogether. For example, Virginia Satir, whom some call the "Mother of Family Therapy," initially used the dramatic context to enact various emotional situations in a family undergoing therapy. In cases where a family member was absent, she would simply involve another group participant to obtain a more comprehensive and dramatic picture. During group psychotherapeutic dramatic interactions, Satir focused less on spontaneity and improvisation. More often, she authoritatively established fixed positions for each participant in the therapeutic enactment and determined the speech constructs that one participant had to express to another. Occasionally, during the process, she would begin explaining the fundamental dynamics of the present moment and the specific changes that might be necessary for the psychotherapeutic changes to take effect. In the vast majority of cases, Satir utilized her dramatic method to resolve family conflicts.

Family constellations, developed by German psychotherapist Bert Hellinger, are essentially a synthesis of Jacob Moreno's psychodrama, Virginia Satir's "family sculpture," Arthur Janov's primal therapy, Milton Erickson's hypnotherapy, Kurt Lewin's group dynamics, Rupert Sheldrake's morphic field concepts, and more. In this case, we can observe the relative integrative nature of the method, but despite the various forms of theoretical and practical borrowing, the actual approach differs radically from its predecessors in many ways. The therapeutic "play" itself, in the vast majority of cases, relies on a subtle sensitivity to the roles played by the "representatives" or actors involved. Based on the information derived from the movement and sensations of the actors, the psychotherapist employs various therapeutic techniques. Sometimes, the approach can be highly directive, with the therapist dictating most of the changes according to certain principles. In other cases, the dynamics of the dramatic constellation within the group itself can serve as a model for non-directive psychotherapeutic work.The pharmaceutical vector encompasses the methodology of pharmacological treatment for various neurotic and psychotic disorders in modern medicine. Different medications are used to address a multitude of psychiatric symptoms. The full development of pharmacotherapy, which enabled the creation of various therapeutic drugs, occurred only in the mid-20th century. Prior to the 1950s, in medical practice for the treatment of mentally ill individuals and the alleviation of various neurotic and psychotic disorders, various plant-based preparations were predominantly used, such as opiates, cocaine, belladonna, and henbane. Non-plant substances such as bromides, internal calcium administration, lithium salts, antihistamines, and others were also popular. In the majority of cases, the use of pharmaceutical agents does not cure the underlying mental disorder but helps manage its symptoms and aids in the patient's socialization. Occasionally, an extended period of symptom control can assist the patient in normalizing their internal mental processes. However, it is all too common to witness individuals suffering from certain disorders who are compelled to take these medications for many years, even decades. Unfortunately, the current development of this vector does not allow for the creation of substances that effectively treat the disorder. Nevertheless, despite some negative aspects associated with the use of pharmaceutical agents, countless patients would not be able to lead even remotely normal lives without them. Furthermore, the application of these agents is often the only means to stabilize a patient's condition to a level where other psychotherapeutic methods can be applied.

The psychedelic vector encompasses theories and practical methods focused on the clinical use of substances that alter the patient's state of consciousness.

The post-psychedelic method describes therapeutic approaches that have evolved from psychedelic methods but no longer rely on chemical means to alter the patient's state of consciousness.

Integrative Therapy

This vector in psychotherapy focuses on integrating various fragmented pieces of therapeutic knowledge into a cohesive whole. At times, these fragments may inherently contradict each other at a theoretical level. When we speak of integration, we mean creating a new organized integrity from fragments of other theories and practices. In this case, the quote by martial arts master Bruce Lee, the creator of Jeet Kune Do, is highly applicable: "Absorb what is useful, discard what is not, and add what is uniquely your own."

The creators of Neuro-Linguistic Programming (NLP), Richard Bandler and John Grinder, as well as their colleagues and students, have come closest to embodying such a philosophy. Over the past 40 years, they have actively developed this approach to psychotherapy and transformed it into something greater than just psychotherapy. However, in NLP, the idea of integration was never postulated as an end in itself.

One key advocate of integration in various fields of science, religion, and specifically psychotherapy is Ken Wilber. His ideas have laid the foundation for an integrative theory that can be effectively utilized in an interdisciplinary context.

On the other hand, if we consider the philosophy of an eclectic approach, it implies using various theoretical concepts and practices in psychotherapy without attempting to unify them into a specific, comprehensive system.

Applicability of Psychopathological Profiles

In the ***Psychology and Psychotherapy: Theories and Practices*** series, I will provide a brief analysis of how the method can be applied to patients with various psychopathological profiles. These profiles often impact the effectiveness of a specific therapeutic approach.

It would be inaccurate to claim that specific methods can only be effective with individuals of a particular profile. However, practical experience indicates that certain patient personality traits are more amenable to change when specific methods are utilized.

Understanding the greater or lesser applicability of different psychotherapy vectors can help foster integrative thinking among psychotherapists, without limiting the practice to methods that may only be fully applicable in certain cases.

I will provide an analysis through the prism of eight **psychopathological profiles**:

1. **Hysteroid** Profile
2. **Paranoid** Profile
3. **Psychopathic** Profile
4. **Obsessive-Compulsive** Profile

5. **Schizoid** Profile
6. **Epileptoid** Profile
7. **Schizophrenic** Profile
8. **Manic-Depressive** Profile

* * *

In the subsequent books of this book series, you will find detailed information on the topics introduced in this first book. ***This first book sets the stage for the series.***

You are about to embark on a journey into the world of modern psychotherapy and the creation of a comprehensive system for understanding patients, methods, and selecting optimal ways of healing and improving the quality of life.

Afterword

In the following books of this series, you will find detailed information about the topics introduced in this first book. *This initial book sets the foundation for the entire series.*

In this book, I have provided a brief overview of the main fundamental directions in psychotherapy. I have explored the key and foundational concepts of many authors that have direct and indirect relevance to psychotherapy.

Each book in the series, dedicated to a specific psychotherapeutic approach, will always be accompanied by an examination of the combination of the therapeutic approach and various psychopathological profiles. Information about psychopathological profiles is presented in a condensed form as it goes beyond the scope of this series.

In the future, I will dedicate a separate, comprehensive work to psychopathological profiling, which will serve as an excellent complement to the information presented in this book.

Certain comprehensive topics have intentionally been deferred to future books in the series, such as psychoanalytic and behavioral vectors, among others. This has been done to create new focal points in the work and emphasize the themes of this series that are rarely mentioned in introductory textbooks on psychotherapy. These include provocative therapy, psychedelic therapy, anti-psychiatry, and others.

Whether this is viewed as good or bad is for the reader to

decide. However, I have made every effort to make this work truly engaging and informative.

The information presented in the books in this series and subsequent ones is structured in our perception into a specific three-dimensional model. This model allows for easy and rapid utilization of information, understanding its specificity, and capturing the interconnections between its various parts.

Some vectors have been discussed in this series, while others will be addressed in the next one. Additionally, future plans include adding supplements to the vectors already presented in this work.

Psychotherapy Vectors Model

Behavioral Vector	Provocative Vector	Cognitive Vector
Psychoanalytic Vector	Integrative Vector	Hypnotic Vector
Somatic Vector	Humanistic Vector	Existential Vector

Table 1

Drama Therapy	Integrative Vector	Pharmaceutical Vector

Table 2

This is the basic three-dimensional model of psychotherapy vectors, with the integrative vector of psychotherapy as the central intersecting point. In the introduction, we have already discussed the dichotomy of psychotherapy vectors, which you can clearly see in the context of this model.

Thus, in our work, we have not only attempted to explore the spectrum of psychotherapy schools but also specifically organize them in relation to each other. In my opinion, this creates the opportunity to effectively and systematically memorize, store, and utilize the information that has been read and accumulated.

This method of structuring through the prism of a three-dimensional model has evolved over many years. During the course on the fundamentals of psychotherapy in universities, the foundation was laid for our understanding of which information would be more effective in presentation and which would not. Over the years, the course has undergone numerous changes as we constantly strive to improve it, making it more practical and engaging. The outcome of our work is a private school of psychotherapy where I have shaped knowledge into a comprehensive structural model. What you will find in "*Psychology and Psychotherapy: Theories and Practices*" series is only a part of this structural model, which encompasses many other important topics that, in my view, are necessary for a systematic understanding of psychotherapy and comprehensive education.

I hope that this work will lead to a new understanding of what psychotherapy is, the various branches it encompasses, and their distinctive features.

* * *

The following psychotherapy approaches will be discussed in the books of the *Psychology and Psychotherapy: Theories and Practices* series:

1. *Psychotherapy Introduction*
2. *Provocative Therapy*
3. *Humanistic Therapy*
4. *Somatic Therapy*
5. *Existential Therapy*
6. *Drama Therapy*
7. *Psychedelic Therapy*
8. *Beyond Psychiatry*
9. *Integrative Therapy*

   ***Psychotherapy Fundamentals* (Books 1-9 Complete Set)**

10. *Theory & History of Hypnosis*
11. *Hypnotherapy Training*

    ***Hypnotherapy Fundamentals* (Books 10-11 Complete Set)**

12. *Psychology of Love and Death*
13. *Breathwork Therapy Seminar*
14. *Cognitive Behavioral Therapy*

Access author page: books2read.com/Artem-Kudelia-PhD

A Brief Message from the Author

Mastering complex psychotherapeutic theories and practices can be a challenging journey. By sharing your experience with this book, you can guide others who are on the same path. Your review could inspire someone to take the next step in deepening their knowledge and applying these insights to make meaningful changes in their life.

Thank you for your support and for taking the time to share your thoughts! Your feedback helps us refine our offerings and empowers others in their pursuit of mastering psychotherapy. If this book has been valuable to you, I'd be grateful if you could take a moment to leave a review. **Your positive rating would mean a lot!**

To share your feedback, simply scan the QR code or click the link below:

psychemaster.com/recommends/review-psychotherapy-introduction

About the Author

Dr. **Artem Kudelia**, a psychologist with a PhD and a practicing therapist, has extensive expertise in integrative approaches. He possesses comprehensive knowledge of a wide range of psychotherapeutic methods, including humanistic and existential theories, as well as the practical application of cognitive-behavioral therapy (CBT) to effectively address issues such as anxiety, depression, obsessive thoughts, compulsions, social phobias, and complex emotions. His books are valuable resources for professionals and individuals interested in managing their mental health. In addition to managing symptoms, he helps his clients toward self-actualization in various aspects of their lives, including social, career, and personal aspects.

You can connect with me on:

- https://facebook.com/psyche.masters
- https://instagram.com/psyche.masters
- https://threads.net/@psyche.masters
- https://youtube.com/@psyche.masters
- https://tiktok.com/@psyche.masters
- https://pinterest.com/psychemasters

Subscribe to my newsletter:

https://psychemaster.com/early-reader-signup

Also by Artem Kudelia PhD

The ***Psychology & Psychotherapy Theories & Practices*** series offers a detailed examination of the history, theoretical foundations, and practical applications of fundamental approaches in psychotherapy. It is an indispensable resource for psychologists, medical professionals, psychology students, and anyone interested in understanding these complex subjects.

Additionally, the ***Cognitive Behavioral Therapy Self-Help Guide: 15 Steps to Mental Health*** series provides actionable guidance for overcoming various psychological challenges, such as anxiety, depression, excessive anger, obsessive thoughts, compulsions, social phobias, health anxiety, and intricate emotional struggles. These topics were chosen because many individuals facing these challenges often lack awareness of the underlying dynamics. By gaining insight into these processes, individuals can make informed decisions about seeking help, reinforcing the idea that knowledge is a powerful tool for personal empowerment.

Together, these series offer invaluable resources for those interested in psychology, whether for academic study or personal development, by providing comprehensive insights and practical tools that contribute to improved mental well-being.

Psychotherapy Fundamentals Complete Guide

Are you struggling to understand complex psychotherapeutic theories?

Psychotherapy Fundamentals: Complete Guide simplifies the intricate world of psychotherapy, making it accessible and actionable for those interested in self-discovery, self-education, and readers with a wide range of interests.

♥ Imagine confidently navigating psychotherapeutic real-world scenarios with ease.

This book is your *comprehensive roadmap to achieving a deep and practical understanding of psychotherapy*. You'll learn to simplify complex theories and integrate them effectively into your life and practice.

Gain a comprehensive understanding of various therapeutic approaches, including *provocative* therapy, *humanistic* therapy, *somatic* therapy, *existential* therapy, *drama* therapy, *psychedelic* and *post-psychedelic* therapy, *anti-psychiatric* therapy, and *integrative* therapy. Each chapter delves into the key themes and methods of these psychotherapy modalities, broadening the horizons for those interested in self-discovery, self-education, and lifelong learning.

▼

https://books2read.com/Psychotherapy-Fundamentals

Hypnotherapy Fundamentals Complete Guide

Are you ready to uncover the secrets of hypnotherapy?

This comprehensive guide immerses you in the ***theory*** *and history of hypnosis*, providing a solid foundation for understanding the principles underlying hypnotherapy.

Explore the various techniques and approaches used in *hypnotherapy* ***training*** through ***practice exercises***, including the art of *suggestion* and deepening *hypnotic trance states*, the creation of therapeutic propositions, and the utilization of the power of the subconscious mind.

Learn how to effectively apply *hypnotherapy techniques* to address a wide range of issues, from managing stress and anxiety to overcoming phobias and habits.

Gain an understanding of the transformative potential of hypnosis and its applications for personal growth and well-being.

Unlock the secrets of harnessing the power of the mind and creating positive changes in yourself and others.

https://books2read.com/Hypnotherapy-Fundamentals

Psychology of Love & Death
Therapeutic Path to Fundamental Balance in Life and Relationships

How to Achieve Fundamental Balance in Life and Relationships?

Explore dualistic nature of human consciousness, along with the profound impact of seeking balance between fundamental continuums of *love and death*, *instinct and spirituality, masculinity and femininity* in shaping our experiences and relationships.

Explore the psychopathological profiles and manifestations of love and death, including profiles such as hysteria, paranoia, psychopathy, and others.

Uncover different types of love, from eros to agape, and study the *three-component Theory of Love.*

Familiarize yourself with *real-life psychotherapy cases* that illustrate the complexities of love, death, and therapy and gain *valuable insights* into the human experience and its challenges.

https://books2read.com/Psychology-of-Love-and-Death

Breathwork Therapy Seminar
Holotropic Journey to Unconscious Mind Secrets

Tap Into the Wisdom of Transpersonal Psychology!

This book is the transcript of a seminar that addresses the profound questions of *subconsciousness*, offering a unique perspective on personal growth and healing.

Gain profound insights into the workings of your mind and explore the mysteries of human consciousness.

Access practical exercises and *techniques* to facilitate personal growth, healing, and self-awareness through *breathwork.*

Written for seekers of self-awareness, psychology enthusiasts, and anyone curious about the depths of the human mind.

Explore the integration of spirituality and psychology, uncovering your inner potential.

▼

https://books2read.com/Breathwork-Therapy

Cognitive Behavioral Therapy
Managing Anxiety and Depression

Explore the roots of anxiety and learn why it's a fundamental aspect of the human experience.

An in-depth exploration of *Panic Disorder*, addressing the irrational fears associated with it.

Examine the nuances of *Social Anxiety* and its impact on personal and professional spheres.

Dive into the world of *Obsessive-Compulsive Disorder*, unraveling its complexities.

Understand the genetic predispositions and learn effective strategies to manage obsessions and compulsions.

Explore *PTSD* from its roots to its biological manifestations. Delve into the trauma cycles, and discover therapeutic techniques for stabilization and overcoming trauma.

Grasp the degrees of *Depression*, from mild to severe, debunking common myths.

▼

https://books2read.com/Cognitive-Behavioral-Therapy

Psychotherapy
Introduction to Healing Vectors

Do you want to understand the variety of methods of psychotherapy and choose the one that is best for you?

In the vast world of psycho-technologies, there are numerous methods of psychotherapy that encompass a wide range of *personality theories* and concepts.

Drawing upon an integral framework, the book maps out the complex *landscape of psychotherapy*, encompassing vectors such as *psychoanalytic*, *hypnotic*, *provocative*, *humanistic*, *behavioral*, *existential*, *transpersonal*, *cognitive*, *somatic*, *psychodramatic* and *psychedelic* therapies, among many others.

This book will provide you with valuable knowledge that will allow you to choose the most suitable therapeutic path for specific circumstances and personality types.

▼

https://books2read.com/Psychotherapy-Introduction

Provocative Therapy
The Healing Power of Dark Humor

Who said that psychotherapy can't be hilariously funny?

Explore innovative ideas about the power of humor in psychotherapy and coaching.

Uncover the archetypal foundation of Provocative Therapy inspired by the myths of the Trickster and the Holy Fool.

Delve into the transformational potential of *Group Provocative Psychotherapy* and the important rules that define successful group dynamics.

Explore the effectiveness of *Provocative Coaching* and its focus points.

Dive into the fascinating world of *Provocative Drama* and its role in therapeutic interventions.

Explore the *pathopsychological profiles*, including *hysteroid, paranoid, psychopathic, obsessive-compulsive, schizoid, epileptoid, schizophrenic,* and *manic-depressive* profiles.

▼

https://books2read.com/Provocative-Therapy

Humanistic Therapy
From Crisis to Self-Actualization

Do you want to explore a world where people are seen as unique holistic systems with infinite potential waiting to be discovered?

Immerse yourself in the theories and practices of humanistic therapy and explore the *transformative path from crisis to self-actualization.*

Unlike psychoanalysis, which focuses on internal complexes and personal traumas, humanistic therapy emphasizes the *study and development of positive personality qualities.*

Humanistic philosophy has also influenced fields such as *education*, promoting *empathy* and *support* as the foundation of learning.

This holistic approach recognizes the *interconnectedness of mind, body, and spirit* and seeks to stimulate personal *growth* and *well-being.*

Take the first step towards self-awareness, personal growth, and a more fulfilling existence.

https://books2read.com/Humanistic-Therapy

Somatic Therapy
The Wisdom of the Body

Would you like to establish a connection with your body and access the source of wisdom?

Unleash the transformative power of *somatic therapy* and embark on a journey of *self-discovery* and *healing.*

Explore the profound connection between the *mind and body.*

Discover the *seven levels of muscular armor* and their connection to specific emotions such as sadness, anger, and fear.

By exploring different body segments, you will unlock *powerful techniques* for releasing pent-up emotions and promoting harmony throughout the organism. From *eye movements* and *jaw exercises* to *deep breathing* and *body movements*, this book offers *practical methods* for *accessing the wisdom of the body* and *restoring emotional balance.*

Acquire unique knowledge about *healing after birth trauma and psychosomatic medicine.*

▼

https://books2read.com/Somatic-Therapy

Existential Therapy
Journey to Authenticity

Do you want to know who you really are? What is your personal meaning of existence?

Embark on a *transformative journey* to uncover your *true essence* and embrace the *principles* of existential therapy.

Explore the rich philosophical roots of *existential psychotherapy* and find your path to *personal authenticity.*

Explore key themes such as *freedom, responsibility, meaning,* and *choice*, and learn to courageously and authentically navigate the complexities of existence.

This book provides *practical ideas and techniques* for *applying the principles of existential therapy* to your own life.

Gain a deep *understanding* of your *values, beliefs*, and *desires*, and learn to *embrace uncertainty* and *transform* life's *challenges* into *opportunities* for *growth* and *self-discovery.*

▼

https://books2read.com/Existential-Therapy

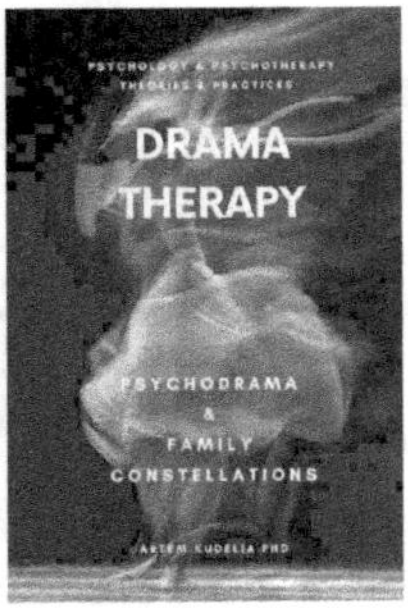

Drama Therapy
Potential of Psychodrama and Family Constellations

Explore the unique world of drama therapeutic approach!

Therapeutic model of intervention that encompasses 12 *powerful speech patterns* capable of significantly *influencing conscious and unconscious processes.*

Through *psychodramatic techniques* and *family constellations*, you will *gain practical knowledge* to enhance your therapeutic practice.

Addressing a wide spectrum of *psychopathological profiles*, including *hysteria, paranoia*, and *obsessive-compulsive disorders*, this book equips you with effective dramatherapeutic activities and psychodynamic exercises.

It serves as a *comprehensive guide* to *crisis intervention, counseling theory*, and *strategies for addiction rehabilitation.*

Gain an understanding of the right hemisphere and the *neuroscience* underlying drama therapy, and learn to *navigate complex emotional situations* with *understanding* and *acceptance.*

https://books2read.com/Drama-Therapy-Constellations

Psychedelic Therapy
The Healing Power Therapeutic Journeys

Embark on a transformative journey into the world of psychedelic therapy!

Explore the fascinating *history* of *psychedelic substances* and potential benefits of working with consciousness-altering substances in clinical practice.

Learn comprehensive information on various *psychedelic therapies*, including *ketamine therapy*, *psilocybin*-assisted psychotherapy, *MDMA*-assisted psychotherapy, and *ibogaine* psychotherapy.

Gain knowledge about *mental health* in the *perinatal period*, the *role of hypnosis*, and the transformative power of *holotropic breathwork*.

Understand the profound impact of *psychedelic medicine* and the potential of *psilocybin microdosing*.

Explore the therapeutic applications of *ketamine* in the *treatment of depression* and *psychosynthesis in coaching*.

https://books2read.com/Psychedelic-Therapy-Journey

Beyond Psychiatry
Exploring Anti-Psychiatry Method

Challenge traditional psychiatry and psychotherapy!

This book presents an *alternative to conventional* ideas of normalcy and offers a *fresh perspective on psychological disorders*, inviting readers to question existing paradigms.

Delve deeper into *psychopathological profiles* and *anti-psychiatric* forms of psychotherapy, examining various profiles including *hysteria, paranoia, psychopathy*, and more.

Gain an understanding of the intersection of psychotherapy and existential philosophy, *challenging the myth of mental illness* within families.

Explore the *treatment of psychosis, trauma*, and *emotional disorders from a holistic perspective.*

▼

https://books2read.com/Beyond-Psychiatry

Integrative Therapy
Personal Transformation Guide

Discover the Power of Integrative Therapy and Embark on a Journey of Personal Transformation!

This book challenges traditional divisions in *therapeutic approaches* and explores the potential of *combining multiple vectors* to create a *comprehensive and integrated therapeutic system.*

Immerse yourself in the world of *neuro-linguistic programming* (NLP), *cognitive styles, neurological levels*, and *integral philosophy*, among other concepts.

Explore practical methodologies such as *shifting negative thinking*, *creating rapport*, and using linguistic patterns to facilitate positive change.

Unlock the transformative *power of anchors*, *changing personal history* and *submodalities.*

Gain an understanding of maps of the world and the *metamodel* for *effective communication.*

https://books2read.com/Integrative-Therapy

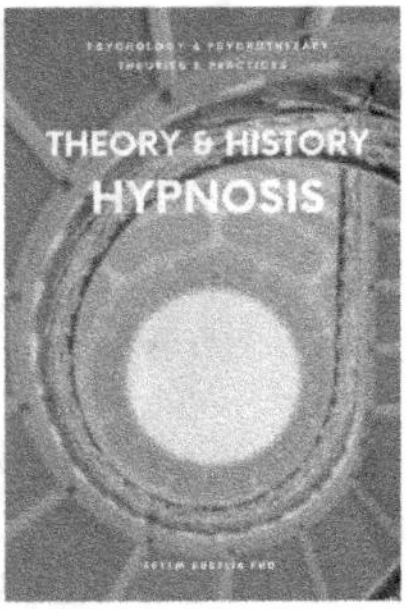

Theory & History of Hypnosis
Exploring Altered State of Mind in Trance

Immerse yourself in the fascinating world of hypnosis and explore the history and theory of altered states of consciousness!

This book sheds light on *historical trance practices* and the *role of shamanism*, tracing its influence on *modern psychospiritual orientations.*

Discover the benefits of this book by exploring the *history of trance practices and hypnotherapy.*

Explore the *evolution* of *shamanism*, its connection to *religion*, and its pre-religious *philosophy*, which offered deep insights into the structure of the universe and the mysteries of the spiritual world.

Discover various *hypnotic phenomena* and *states of consciousness* that can be induced in a trance state.

Explore their potential applications in *psychotherapeutic practice*, from *pain management* to the *treatment of depression.*

Learn techniques such as *self-hypnosis, deep trance induction*, and *guided healing visualizations.*

▼

https://books2read.com/Theory-and-History-of-Hypnosis

Hypnotherapy Training
A Guide for Practicing Hypnotherapists

Uncover the secrets of hypnotherapy and improve your practical hypnosis skills!

This book explores *techniques* and *practical skills* for hypnotherapists.

Dive into the depths of the *subconscious* and discover the *transformative potential* of hypnotherapy.

Discover the benefits of this book, which delves into key topics and approaches in *hypnotherapy training.*

Explore developed techniques, including rapport-building practices and the use of matching postures, movements, and breathing with the client.

Engage in exercises that enable the attainment of different trance levels and explore the motives of trance and their application in psychotherapy.

Gain an understanding of different styles and orientations of hypnotic work, from hypnoanalytic and suggestive to behavioral and transpersonal.

▼

https://books2read.com/Hypnotherapy-Training

Healing Anxiety and Overthinking
Proven CBT Strategies for Lasting Relief

Are you exhausted from the relentless cycle of anxiety and overthinking?

Discover the 15-step program that will transform your mental health and bring peace of mind.

Millions of adults struggle with anxiety and overthinking, feeling trapped in a cycle of worry and stress. But it doesn't have to be this way. "*Healing Anxiety and Overthinking: Proven CBT Strategies for Lasting Relief*" offers a comprehensive guide to breaking free from the grip of anxiety using practical, proven **Cognitive Behavioral Therapy** (**CBT**) strategies.

♥ ***Imagine waking up every day with a clear mind, free from the constant barrage of anxious thoughts***

This book is your roadmap to achieving that transformation in just 15 steps. You'll learn to understand the nature of your anxiety, identify its triggers, and apply effective techniques to manage and overcome it.

Take Control of Your Mental Health

Don't let anxiety and overthinking rule your life. With "*Healing Anxiety and Overthinking,*" you'll gain the tools and confidence to achieve peace of mind and live the life you deserve.

Mastering Intrusive Thoughts
Practical CBT Techniques for Managing OCD

*Is **OCD** ruling your life with intrusive thoughts and compulsions?*

Take back control with scientifically-proven CBT techniques designed to help you regain peace of mind.

Millions of adults struggle with obsessive-compulsive disorder (OCD), caught in a relentless cycle of intrusive thoughts and compulsive behaviors. "Mastering Intrusive Thoughts" is your step-by-step guide to breaking free from the grip of OCD using practical, evidence-based Cognitive Behavioral Therapy (CBT) techniques.

♥ ***Picture yourself waking up with a calm, focused mind, no longer burdened by the constant anxiety of unwanted thoughts.***

In this book, Dr. Artem Kudelia offers a clear and actionable path to mastering your thoughts in 15 manageable steps. Whether you're new to CBT or have tried other methods without success, this guide provides the tools you need to finally achieve relief.

✔ Take the First Step Towards Mental Freedom

You'll gain the knowledge and confidence to conquer your **OCD** and reclaim your peace of mind.

The Anger Solution
A CBT Program for Emotional Balance

Are you tired of living with persistent anger and overwhelming stress?

Discover a practical, 15-step program designed to bring lasting peace and transform your emotional health.

Millions of adults struggle with anger and stress, feeling trapped in a cycle of frustration and tension. But it doesn't have to be this way. "The Anger Solution" offers a comprehensive guide to breaking free from the grip of anger using practical, proven Cognitive Behavioral Therapy (CBT) strategies.

❤ ***Imagine waking up every day with a calm mind, free from the constant barrage of anger and stress.***

This book is your roadmap to achieving that transformation. With clear, actionable steps, you'll learn to understand the nature of your anger, identify its triggers, and apply effective techniques to manage and overcome it.

✔ Take Control of Your Emotional Health

With "The Anger Solution," you'll gain the tools and confidence to achieve emotional balance and live the life you deserve.

Health Anxiety Mastery
30 Proven CBT Steps to Peace of Mind

Is health anxiety controlling your life with constant worry and fear?

Regain peace of mind with proven CBT techniques designed to help you overcome health-related anxiety and reclaim control.

Millions of people struggle with health anxiety, trapped in a cycle of physical symptoms, endless reassurance-seeking, and intrusive thoughts about their well-being. "*Health Anxiety Mastery*" offers a clear, step-by-step approach to breaking free from these patterns using practical, evidence-based Cognitive Behavioral Therapy (CBT) techniques.

♥ **Imagine waking up each day calm and confident, no longer overwhelmed by fear and obsessive thoughts about your health.**

In this book, you'll find 30 actionable steps to help you reduce anxiety, challenge limiting beliefs, and develop healthier thought patterns. Whether you're just beginning your journey or have tried other approaches without success, these practical tools will guide you toward lasting relief.

✔ **Start Your Journey to Balanced Mental Health**

How to Get Over Social Anxiety
CBT Strategies for True Confidence and Deep Connection

What if 15 proven steps could free you from social anxiety and help you connect?

Uncover a 15-step CBT program to overcome fear, stop avoidance, and build true self-confidence. Millions struggle with social anxiety, but you don't have to face it alone. This guide provides a clear, evidence-based path to transforming your social life and connecting authentically.

♥ **Imagine engaging in conversations fearlessly and forming genuine relationships free from judgment or rejection.**

With insights from proven cognitive-behavioral techniques and relatable examples, this book offers the practical tools and encouragement needed to face your fears and succeed socially.

✔ **Begin Your Journey to Confidence**

Start transforming fear into connection and reclaim control of your social life with "*How to Get Over Social Anxiety.*"

Discover More by Artem Kudelia

Scan the QR code or click the link to access his author page and full collection. Each book provides detailed insights and practical guidance, exemplifying his contributions to psychology and psychotherapy.

books2read.com/Artem-Kudelia-PhD

www.ingramcontent.com/pod-product-compliance
Lightning Source LLC
LaVergne TN
LVHW022017200926
848481LV00007B/2444